PRINCEWILL LAGANG

The Role of Friendship in a Romantic Relationship

First published by PRINCEWILL LAGANG 2023

Copyright © 2023 by Princewill Lagang

All rights reserved. No part of this publication may be reproduced, stored or transmitted in any form or by any means, electronic, mechanical, photocopying, recording, scanning, or otherwise without written permission from the publisher. It is illegal to copy this book, post it to a website, or distribute it by any other means without permission.

Princewill Lagang asserts the moral right to be identified as the author of this work.

First edition

This book was professionally typeset on Reedsy.
Find out more at reedsy.com

Contents

1. Introduction — 1
2. The Foundation of Friendship — 4
3. Shared Interests and Activities — 7
4. Open Communication and Trust — 10
5. Playfulness and Laughter — 13
6. Emotional Support and Empathy — 16
7. Navigating Challenges Together — 19
8. Balancing Togetherness and Independence — 22
9. Adventure and Exploration — 25
10. Growth and Evolution — 28
11. Communication and Conflict Resolution — 31
12. Embracing the Friendship-Romance Connection — 34

1

Introduction

In the realm of romantic relationships, the intertwining of friendship and love has long been a subject of intrigue and contemplation. This chapter delves into the theme of friendship within romantic relationships and explores the crucial significance of examining how friendship serves as a cornerstone of love. As human connections continually evolve and redefine themselves, understanding the dynamics of friendship and love has never been more pertinent.

The concept of friendship within romantic relationships suggests a harmonious blend of emotional intimacy and companionship. Traditionally, love and friendship have often been viewed as separate entities, each with its own distinct characteristics. However, recent shifts in societal norms and relationship paradigms have prompted a reevaluation of this demarcation. Couples are increasingly recognizing that a strong foundation of friendship can underpin profound and enduring romantic love. As such, exploring the dimensions of this unique intersection becomes an exciting avenue for inquiry.

At its core, this study aims to unravel the multifaceted ways in which friendship enriches romantic relationships. Friendship, characterized by mutual trust, open communication, shared interests, and genuine care, introduces a layer of authenticity that transcends the romantic realm. This authenticity, in turn, nurtures the emotional connection between partners, creating a bond that extends beyond passion and physical attraction. By examining the interplay between friendship and love, we can gain insights into how these relationships weather challenges, foster personal growth, and sustain long-term happiness.

Central to this exploration is the recognition of the importance of understanding how friendship contributes to the overarching concept of love. Love, often seen as an amalgamation of various emotions and desires, takes on a richer and more nuanced hue when seen through the lens of friendship. The emotional safety and comfort that a true friend provides can serve as a crucible for love to flourish. Moreover, the absence of friendship can leave romantic relationships vulnerable to superficiality and transitory infatuation.

Intriguingly, the dynamic between friendship and love is not a one-size-fits-all construct. Each relationship is an intricate tapestry woven by the unique personalities, experiences, and aspirations of the individuals involved. Therefore, this study seeks to illuminate the diverse ways in which friendship may manifest within romantic partnerships. Whether it be the slow evolution from friends to lovers, the integration of long-standing friendships into romantic connections, or the discovery of newfound friendship within an established romantic bond, the exploration of these pathways promises to uncover compelling narratives.

In conclusion, this chapter introduces the captivating theme of friendship within romantic relationships and underscores the critical importance of investigating the ways in which friendship contributes to the foundation of love. By delving into the depths of this symbiotic relationship, we embark on a journey that transcends the conventional boundaries of romance, offering a profound understanding of human connections and the intricate forces that

INTRODUCTION

shape them.

2

The Foundation of Friendship

In the landscape of romantic partnerships, friendship stands as a cornerstone that underpins the very essence of enduring love. This chapter delves into the pivotal role that friendship assumes within romantic relationships, exploring its definition, characteristics, and how it complements and enriches the fabric of romantic love.

Defining Friendship within Romantic Partnerships

Friendship, commonly understood as a bond between individuals built on trust, shared experiences, mutual understanding, and a sense of companionship, takes on new dimensions when interwoven with romantic love. In a romantic context, friendship extends beyond mere camaraderie; it involves a deeper emotional connection that transcends fleeting infatuation or physical attraction. This unique blend of familiarity and intimacy forms the bedrock upon which romantic relationships thrive.

Characteristics of Friendship in Romantic Love

The qualities that define friendship—trust, communication, shared interests, and genuine care—are amplified when interwoven with romantic love. Trust, a foundational aspect of any friendship, takes on heightened importance in a romantic context. Partners share their vulnerabilities, confide their fears and aspirations, and find solace in each other's unwavering support. This emotional transparency fosters a level of intimacy that is essential for the growth and sustainability of romantic relationships.

Effective communication, another hallmark of friendship, finds even greater significance in romantic partnerships. The ability to express feelings, thoughts, and concerns openly ensures that misunderstandings are minimized and conflicts are resolved in a healthy manner. This willingness to engage in heartfelt conversations nurtures a connection that transcends surface-level interactions, forming the basis for lasting romantic love.

Shared interests and common values, often celebrated in friendships, serve as a bridge connecting partners on a deeper level. The joy of engaging in activities together, pursuing mutual passions, and aligning life goals solidifies the friendship-based foundation of the relationship. These shared experiences create a reservoir of cherished memories that bolster the emotional bond between partners.

Complementary Nature of Friendship and Romantic Love

Friendship and romantic love, far from being mutually exclusive, complement and enhance each other in remarkable ways. While romantic love may spark the initial attraction and passion, it is friendship that sustains and fortifies the relationship over time. The deep level of companionship, emotional intimacy, and trust that friendship offers aligns seamlessly with the multifaceted nature of romantic love.

Furthermore, friendship introduces an element of security and comfort that acts as a buffer against the challenges that all relationships inevitably face. Couples who view each other as friends, in addition to being romantic partners, tend to navigate conflicts more constructively and approach challenges with a united front. The friendship-based foundation fosters empathy and a willingness to support each other's personal growth, allowing the relationship to adapt and evolve over time.

In conclusion, this chapter elucidates the foundational role of friendship within romantic relationships. By defining the characteristics that distinguish friendship in a romantic context, it becomes evident that friendship acts as a catalyst for emotional intimacy, effective communication, shared experiences, and lasting trust. The intrinsic harmony between friendship and romantic love illustrates their complementary nature, painting a compelling portrait of partnerships that thrive on the synergy between these two profound forms of human connection.

3

Shared Interests and Activities

Shared Interests and Activities: Catalysts for Friendship and Bond Strengthening

In the intricate tapestry of romantic relationships, shared interests and activities emerge as dynamic threads that not only foster friendship but also weave a stronger, more resilient bond between partners. This chapter embarks on a journey to uncover the pivotal role that shared hobbies and passions play in cultivating friendship within romantic partnerships. It delves into the ways in which engaging in activities together enhances emotional connection, nurtures understanding, and contributes to the overall depth of love.

The Role of Shared Interests in Fostering Friendship

Shared interests serve as a bridge that transcends the boundaries of everyday life, creating common ground upon which couples can build a profound sense of companionship. Engaging in activities that both partners are passionate about fosters a sense of unity and shared purpose. This shared purpose extends beyond the individual realm and forms a basis for mutual understanding and emotional connection.

Through shared interests, couples find themselves in an environment where they can comfortably express themselves, communicate openly, and collaborate harmoniously. This organic exchange of ideas and experiences nurtures the core elements of friendship—trust, empathy, and a sense of camaraderie—while simultaneously enhancing the romantic dimension of the relationship.

Engaging in Hobbies Together: Strengthening the Bond

Participating in hobbies and activities together presents a unique opportunity for partners to bond on a deeper level. The act of learning, exploring, and enjoying new experiences as a team fosters a sense of adventure and novelty that keeps the relationship dynamic and exciting. This shared adventure serves as a conduit for creating memories that are not only cherished but also serve as touchstones for future interactions.

Furthermore, the process of engaging in hobbies often requires collaboration, problem-solving, and compromise. These qualities, vital in both friendships and romantic partnerships, are honed and refined as couples work together to achieve common goals. The challenges faced and conquered while pursuing shared interests solidify the sense of partnership, reaffirming the bond that holds the relationship together.

Enhancing Emotional Connection and Understanding

Shared interests and activities provide a unique avenue for partners to connect emotionally and deepen their understanding of one another. Engaging in activities that hold personal significance for each individual allows them to share a piece of themselves with their partner. This vulnerability and willingness to be authentic create a strong foundation of trust and emotional intimacy.

Moreover, shared interests can offer insights into each partner's values, aspirations, and preferences. Through these activities, couples gain a deeper understanding of what makes each other tick, thereby fostering empathy and compassion. This heightened emotional connection paves the way for effective communication, as partners become attuned to each other's needs and desires.

In conclusion, this chapter illuminates the powerful role of shared interests and activities in nurturing friendship and reinforcing the bond within romantic relationships. By engaging in hobbies together, couples create spaces of unity, adventure, and emotional connection. These shared experiences serve as vehicles for understanding, empathy, and growth, solidifying the friendship-based foundation of the partnership while enhancing the romantic love that flourishes within it.

4

Open Communication and Trust

Open Communication and Trust: The Cornerstones of Friendship and Beyond

Within the intricate architecture of romantic relationships, open communication and trust emerge as the bedrock upon which friendship is forged and the bonds of love are fortified. This chapter delves into the pivotal role of open communication and trust in building the foundation of friendship within romantic partnerships. It explores how these elements shape mutual reliance, emotional intimacy, and the profound connections that define successful relationships.

The Power of Open Communication in Building Friendship

Open communication serves as a vital conduit for the development of friendship within romantic partnerships. It is through honest and candid conversations that partners reveal their thoughts, feelings, and vulnerabilities. This transparency not only fosters a sense of emotional intimacy but also lays the groundwork for a genuine understanding of each other's hopes, fears, and dreams.

Engaging in open communication also enables couples to navigate challenges with resilience and unity. When partners feel comfortable expressing their concerns, doubts, and insecurities, they create an environment of mutual support and validation. This open dialogue, free from judgment, becomes an avenue for personal growth and a testament to the friendship-based foundation of the relationship.

Trust: The Keystone of Friendship and Romantic Love

Trust forms the very core of both friendship and romantic love. In friendships, trust is the pillar upon which companions rely when sharing secrets, seeking advice, or seeking refuge. Similarly, in romantic relationships, trust forms the foundation for vulnerability and emotional connection. When partners feel confident that their feelings and vulnerabilities will be respected and protected, they become more willing to open their hearts to one another.

Trust also extends beyond emotional transparency to encompass reliability and dependability. Partners who trust each other implicitly can rely on each other not only as romantic companions but also as friends who are unwavering in their support. This mutual reliability contributes to a sense of security and comfort, strengthening the bond and allowing the relationship to flourish in times of both joy and adversity.

Relying on Each Other as Friends

In cultivating friendship within romantic partnerships, the ability to rely on one another transcends the traditional roles of romantic partners. Just as friends are there to offer a listening ear, provide advice, and stand by each other's side, partners in romantic relationships should similarly extend the hand of friendship. Relying on each other for emotional support, understanding, and encouragement fosters a sense of companionship that enriches the connection.

This reliance also extends to shared decision-making, problem-solving, and goal-setting. Partners who view each other as friends are more likely to collaborate harmoniously, leveraging their mutual trust and open communication to overcome challenges and seize opportunities. This alignment of purpose creates a partnership that is not only built on romance but also on shared values and aspirations.

In conclusion, this chapter underscores the indispensable role of open communication and trust in shaping the foundation of friendship within romantic relationships. The power of honest conversations, emotional transparency, and mutual trust enhances the depth of emotional connection and builds a strong bond. As partners learn to rely on each other as friends, they pave the way for a relationship that thrives on companionship, empathy, and shared growth.

5

Playfulness and Laughter

The Essence of Playfulness and Laughter: Infusing Joy into Romantic Relationships

In the symphony of romantic relationships, playfulness and laughter emerge as delightful notes that harmonize the melodies of companionship and love. This chapter delves into the intrinsic value of playfulness and humor within romantic partnerships, exploring their ability to create a buoyant atmosphere that enhances emotional connection and nurtures lasting bonds. It also offers anecdotes and strategies for infusing joy into relationships, making them more vibrant and resilient.

The Significance of Playfulness and Laughter in Romance

Playfulness and laughter serve as catalysts for forging a unique, lighthearted friendship within romantic relationships. Just as friends share moments of mirth and amusement, romantic partners who engage in playful interactions create an environment that nurtures their emotional connection. Laughter, as a universal language, transcends cultural and linguistic boundaries, enabling partners to communicate and share joy in profound ways.

Incorporating playfulness into the relationship also serves as a reminder of the initial excitement that often accompanies the early stages of romance. The ability to engage in playful banter, inside jokes, and shared laughter rekindles the sense of adventure that accompanies the beginning of a journey together. This shared joy contributes to a sense of unity and solidarity, forming a foundation that can weather challenges and promote long-term happiness.

Anecdotes and Strategies for Infusing Joy

Anecdotes from various romantic partnerships highlight the myriad ways in which playfulness and laughter can be integrated into relationships. Simple acts like surprise pranks, spontaneous dance parties, or engaging in friendly competitions inject an element of fun into everyday life. Sharing humorous anecdotes, reliving funny memories, and creating playful rituals become cherished traditions that underscore the uniqueness of the relationship.

Strategies for infusing joy into partnerships involve embracing spontaneity and creativity. Engaging in shared hobbies, whether it's trying a new recipe, embarking on a spontaneous road trip, or attempting a quirky art project, introduces an element of novelty that keeps the relationship vibrant. Additionally, setting aside designated "playtime" to engage in activities that bring both partners joy ensures that playfulness remains an integral part of the partnership's fabric.

Enhancing Emotional Connection through Laughter

The act of laughter goes beyond surface amusement; it deepens emotional connections by fostering vulnerability and shared experiences. Partners who can laugh together during moments of triumph and adversity cultivate a bond that is built on mutual support and understanding. Sharing a sense of humor allows partners to see each other's authentic selves, dismantling barriers and creating a sense of unity.

Laughter also serves as a powerful coping mechanism during challenging times. Partners who can find humor even in difficult situations demonstrate resilience and a shared perspective that mitigates stress. This ability to navigate life's ups and downs with a touch of levity cements the friendship-based foundation of the relationship, reinforcing the idea that partners can rely on each other in times of both joy and tribulation.

In conclusion, this chapter underscores the profound impact of playfulness and laughter on romantic relationships. By infusing partnerships with moments of joy and shared laughter, couples cultivate a friendship that elevates their emotional connection and strengthens their bond. Whether through playful anecdotes or intentional strategies, embracing a sense of lightheartedness creates a relationship that is characterized by unity, resilience, and enduring companionship.

6

Emotional Support and Empathy

The Heartbeat of Empathy and Emotional Support in Romantic Relationships

In the intricate dance of romantic relationships, the empathetic connection shared between partners evolves as a lifeline of emotional support, breathing life into the very core of companionship. This chapter embarks on an exploration of the profound role that empathy and emotional support play in shaping the friendship within romantic partnerships. It delves into how this connection creates a sanctuary for vulnerability and growth, strengthening the bond that defines enduring love.

Exploring the Empathetic Connection

Empathy serves as a bridge between partners, connecting their emotional worlds and fostering a deep understanding of each other's feelings. In romantic relationships, the empathetic connection extends beyond shared experiences; it involves a willingness to step into each other's shoes, perceive the world through their lens, and offer solace during times of distress. This connection creates an emotional intimacy that solidifies the friendship-based foundation of the partnership.

Empathy, a hallmark of friendship, intertwines harmoniously with the complexities of romantic love. Partners who approach each other's emotions with sensitivity and compassion foster a safe space for vulnerability, where feelings can be freely expressed without fear of judgment or dismissal. This emotional resonance forms a cornerstone upon which a deep sense of companionship is built.

The Strengthening Power of Emotional Support

Emotional support within romantic relationships functions as a lifeline that weaves a bond of trust and solidarity. Just as friends provide a shoulder to lean on during times of turmoil, romantic partners who extend emotional support signal their unwavering commitment to each other's well-being. Offering reassurance, validation, and a listening ear conveys a profound message of "I am here for you."

Emotional support also fosters an environment in which personal growth is nurtured and celebrated. Partners who champion each other's dreams, encourage self-discovery, and provide unwavering support during challenging times create a platform for shared evolution. This supportive camaraderie allows the relationship to flourish as both individuals grow into their best selves.

Creating a Sanctuary for Vulnerability

In friendships, the willingness to reveal one's vulnerabilities forges a deeper connection. Similarly, in romantic partnerships, the ability to share fears, insecurities, and dreams nurtures a profound emotional bond. Partners who offer a safe haven for vulnerability create an environment of trust and intimacy, enriching the connection between friendship and love.

Moreover, emotional support paves the way for effective problem-solving and conflict resolution. Partners who empathize with each other's perspectives are more likely to engage in constructive conversations and seek mutually beneficial resolutions. The ability to navigate challenges with compassion and understanding reinforces the sense of unity and companionship that define lasting relationships.

In conclusion, this chapter underscores the indispensable role of empathy and emotional support in shaping the friendship within romantic relationships. By fostering an empathetic connection, partners create a sanctuary for vulnerability, personal growth, and shared evolution. The act of offering emotional support solidifies the foundation of companionship, promoting a relationship that is rooted in understanding, trust, and enduring love.

7

Navigating Challenges Together

Unified in Adversity: The Power of Friendship-Based Relationships in Overcoming Challenges

In the intricate tapestry of romantic relationships, the friendship-based foundation proves to be an anchor of resilience and unity when facing challenges. This chapter delves into how such relationships handle adversity, offering insights into the dynamics that empower partners to work in tandem, strengthen their bond, and emerge victorious against the tests that life presents.

Challenges and the Friendship-Based Relationship

Challenges, whether they stem from external circumstances or internal dynamics, are an inevitable part of any relationship. What distinguishes friendship-based relationships is the manner in which partners face and navigate these challenges. The presence of friendship fosters an environment where open communication, empathy, and shared goals become pillars of strength in the face of adversity.

Partners who approach challenges with the mindset of friends seek to understand each other's perspectives, acknowledging that both are invested in overcoming the obstacle together. This perspective, rooted in mutual support and understanding, allows the relationship to maintain its stability even in tumultuous times.

Working Together to Overcome Obstacles

Friendship-based relationships thrive on collaboration and problem-solving. Partners who view each other as friends recognize that they are on the same team, united against any challenge that comes their way. This unity not only bolsters their emotional connection but also provides a sense of security that empowers them to face challenges head-on.

Effective communication remains a linchpin in overcoming challenges. Partners who engage in open, respectful discussions are more likely to identify the root causes of the challenge and work together to find solutions. The empathy and emotional support that characterize friendship-based relationships allow for an atmosphere of understanding, where partners are encouraged to share their feelings and thoughts without fear of judgment.

Growth and Resilience through Challenges

Challenges, when approached with a friendship-based mindset, can serve as catalysts for growth and resilience. Partners who navigate difficulties together learn to adapt, compromise, and find innovative solutions. This shared experience fosters personal growth and enhances the connection, creating a narrative of overcoming obstacles as a united front.

Moreover, challenges can reaffirm the commitment partners have to each other. Facing difficulties together strengthens the bond, reminding partners why they chose to embark on this journey as friends and lovers. The trust and emotional intimacy fostered by the friendship-based foundation act as the bedrock upon which challenges are surmounted, ensuring that the relationship emerges stronger than before.

In conclusion, this chapter emphasizes the remarkable capacity of friendship-based relationships to overcome challenges. By approaching adversity with open communication, empathy, and a collaborative spirit, partners reinforce their bond and cultivate a sense of unity. Challenges become opportunities for growth, strengthening the relationship and creating a narrative of resilience that speaks to the enduring power of companionship and love.

8

Balancing Togetherness and Independence

Harmony in Individuality: Nurturing Friendship While Maintaining Identity

In the realm of romantic relationships built on a foundation of friendship, the delicate art of balancing togetherness and independence emerges as a defining skill. This chapter delves into the significance of preserving individuality while nurturing the friendship within romantic partnerships. It explores how partners can strike a harmonious balance between shared experiences and personal space, fostering a relationship that thrives on both unity and autonomy.

The Importance of Maintaining Individuality

While the bond of friendship nurtures emotional intimacy and connection, it is equally essential for partners to maintain their individual identities. Preserving one's unique interests, passions, and personal growth endeavors ensures that each partner continues to evolve independently, bringing fresh perspectives and experiences to the relationship. This individuality is what contributes to the dynamic interplay that defines the relationship's vitality.

Friendship-based relationships celebrate the authenticity of each partner. Embracing and respecting individual differences not only enriches the partnership but also reinforces the friendship foundation. Partners who encourage and support each other's pursuits beyond the relationship foster an environment of trust and autonomy, where both can continue to flourish as individuals.

Striking a Healthy Balance

Finding the equilibrium between togetherness and personal space requires conscious effort and communication. Partners who recognize the value of both shared experiences and independent growth are better equipped to navigate this delicate balance. The ability to spend quality time together while also enjoying solitary activities prevents the relationship from becoming stifling or stagnant.

Open communication plays a pivotal role in achieving this balance. Partners who discuss their needs, preferences, and boundaries openly create a roadmap for coexisting harmoniously. This dialogue promotes understanding and ensures that both partners feel heard and respected, fostering an atmosphere of mutual support.

Tips for Finding Harmony

1. Prioritize Communication: Regularly discuss your desires, needs, and boundaries regarding togetherness and personal space. Honesty and transparency create an environment where both partners feel comfortable expressing their expectations.

2. Create Shared Experiences: Engage in activities that you both enjoy, fostering a sense of togetherness. These shared experiences create cherished memories and strengthen the emotional connection.

3. Respect Each Other's Independence: Encourage and celebrate each other's individual pursuits. Partners who support each other's growth outside of the relationship build a foundation of trust and autonomy.

4. Establish Alone Time: Schedule time for personal activities or self-care. This alone time nurtures individuality and prevents feelings of suffocation.

5. Embrace Compromise: Balancing togetherness and independence often requires compromise. Partners who are willing to meet in the middle create a partnership that thrives on flexibility and understanding.

Fostering Unity through Autonomy

In conclusion, this chapter underscores the significance of finding harmony between togetherness and independence within friendship-based relationships. By valuing individuality and open communication, partners create a relationship that thrives on mutual respect and understanding. Striking this balance nurtures both the friendship and romantic aspects of the relationship, allowing partners to grow independently while fostering a deep sense of companionship.

9

Adventure and Exploration

Embarking on Journeys of Friendship: The Role of Adventure in Romantic Relationships

In the rich tapestry of romantic relationships grounded in friendship, the spirit of adventure emerges as a vibrant thread that weaves excitement, shared experiences, and lasting memories into the very fabric of companionship. This chapter delves into the significance of cultivating a sense of adventure within romantic partnerships. It explores how the pursuit of new experiences and exploration not only deepens the friendship but also fuels the fire of love, creating a dynamic and enriched connection.

The Role of Adventure in Fostering Friendship

Adventure is more than just the pursuit of novelty; it is an embodiment of the curiosity, openness, and shared enthusiasm that underpin friendship. Partners who approach life with a sense of adventure exhibit a willingness to step outside their comfort zones, embrace the unknown, and support each other in exploring uncharted territories. This shared spirit of discovery fosters a bond of companionship that thrives on shared anticipation and excitement.

Moreover, adventure introduces an element of playfulness that characterizes true friendships. Couples who embark on new experiences together often find themselves in situations where laughter, spontaneity, and a sense of camaraderie flourish. This shared joy not only enhances the emotional connection but also rejuvenates the relationship by infusing it with an air of lightheartedness.

Creating Lasting Memories Through Exploration

The pursuit of adventure offers fertile ground for the creation of cherished memories that bolster the friendship-based foundation of the relationship. Whether it's exploring new travel destinations, trying out novel hobbies, or embarking on spontaneous road trips, these shared experiences become touchstones that partners can revisit time and again.

The process of exploration requires collaboration and shared decision-making, qualities that are fundamental to both friendship and romantic partnerships. Partners who work together to plan and execute adventurous endeavors build a sense of unity and accomplishment. These experiences not only create memories but also reinforce the notion that, as friends, they can navigate challenges and celebrate triumphs side by side.

Fueling the Flame of Love

The pursuit of adventure adds a layer of dynamism to romantic relationships, fanning the flames of love with each new experience. As partners share in the excitement of discovery, their emotional connection deepens, and their sense of unity strengthens. The unique memories forged through adventurous pursuits become a testament to the journey they are taking together, creating a shared narrative of growth, joy, and companionship.

Adventure also prevents relationships from becoming stagnant or routine. The infusion of novelty and exploration keeps partners engaged and curious, preventing the relationship from losing its sense of magic. Partners who continue to cultivate a sense of adventure are more likely to experience the ebbs and flows of life as a dynamic journey, creating a relationship that is ever-evolving and enduring.

In conclusion, this chapter highlights the profound role of adventure and exploration in nurturing the friendship-based foundation of romantic relationships. By fostering a sense of curiosity, shared enthusiasm, and light-heartedness, partners infuse their connection with vibrancy and excitement. Through the creation of lasting memories and the constant pursuit of novelty, they celebrate the essence of friendship while nurturing a love that is dynamic, enduring, and bound by the spirit of adventure.

10

Growth and Evolution

The Ever-Unfolding Journey: How Friendship-Based Relationships Evolve

In the tapestry of friendship-based romantic relationships, the passage of time weaves threads of growth, transformation, and enduring connection. This chapter delves into the intricate evolution of these relationships over time, exploring how the foundation of friendship facilitates ongoing growth and nurtures a connection that deepens with each passing day.

The Evolution of Friendship-Based Relationships

Friendship-based relationships possess a unique capacity to evolve gracefully, adapting to the changes and challenges that life presents. As partners traverse the journey of life together, their friendship deepens, offering a robust foundation upon which the relationship thrives. The evolution of such relationships is characterized by an organic progression from companionship to emotional intimacy and enduring love.

Over time, partners in friendship-based relationships witness the strengthening of their emotional bond. The empathy, communication, and shared experiences that define their friendship serve as building blocks for a love that is enriched by the passage of time. This evolution highlights the symbiotic nature of friendship and romantic love, as the friendship foundation continually nourishes the growth of the romantic connection.

Ongoing Growth and Adaptation

Friendship-based relationships are marked by a commitment to mutual growth and personal development. As partners grow individually, they bring new facets of themselves into the relationship, ensuring that it remains dynamic and vibrant. This commitment to personal growth not only contributes to the longevity of the partnership but also underscores the enduring nature of their connection.

Partners who view each other as friends are more likely to adapt and navigate the challenges that arise as life unfolds. The sense of unity and companionship forged through friendship enables couples to approach adversity as a team, sharing the burden and celebrating the triumphs together. This shared journey of growth and adaptation reinforces the bond, creating a narrative of resilience and unity.

Deepening Connection and Lasting Love

The evolution of friendship-based relationships is characterized by a deepening of emotional connection and lasting love. As partners continue to share their lives, vulnerabilities, and dreams, the friendship-based foundation becomes an anchor that sustains the relationship. The depth of emotional intimacy cultivated through shared experiences, open communication, and mutual support fosters a sense of companionship that stands the test of time.

Furthermore, the enduring nature of these relationships is a testament to the authenticity of the connection. The friendship-based foundation ensures that partners remain committed not only to the romantic aspect of the relationship but also to the friendship that underpins it. This multifaceted commitment contributes to a relationship that is characterized by unity, growth, and the perpetuation of a vibrant connection.

In conclusion, this chapter underscores the remarkable evolution of friendship-based romantic relationships over time. Through ongoing growth, adaptation, and the deepening of emotional connection, partners create a narrative of enduring companionship and love. The friendship foundation, serving as a steadfast anchor, empowers couples to navigate the journey of life together, celebrating the richness of their shared experiences and nurturing a bond that grows stronger with every passing day.

11

Communication and Conflict Resolution

Navigating Storms with Friend's Eyes: The Role of Friendship in Effective Communication and Conflict Resolution

In the realm of friendship-based romantic relationships, effective communication and conflict resolution emerge as cornerstones of understanding, empathy, and unity. This chapter delves into how the foundation of friendship enriches these aspects of the relationship, exploring the ways in which partners can draw from their friendship to communicate openly and navigate conflicts with compassion.

The Impact of Friendship on Communication

Friendship lends a unique depth to communication within romantic relationships. Partners who view each other as friends naturally gravitate toward open and honest conversations. The emotional intimacy fostered by friendship facilitates a safe space where feelings, thoughts, and concerns can be freely expressed without fear of judgment. This transparency strengthens the emotional connection, allowing partners to develop a shared language of understanding.

The bond of friendship also promotes effective listening. Just as friends actively engage in conversations and value each other's opinions, partners in friendship-based relationships are more likely to give each other their full attention. This attentive listening not only enhances communication but also conveys a sense of validation and respect.

Conflict Resolution Through a Friend's Perspective

Conflict is an inevitable part of any relationship, but the friendship-based foundation equips partners with a unique perspective for resolving disagreements. Viewing each other as friends rather than adversaries reframes conflicts as challenges to be overcome together, rather than battles to be won. This mindset fosters collaboration and encourages partners to approach conflict resolution as a united front.

Partners who embody the qualities of friendship—empathy, respect, and a shared sense of purpose—create an environment where conflicts are approached with a focus on understanding rather than blame. This perspective enables partners to explore the underlying issues, identify common ground, and seek solutions that benefit both parties.

Strategies for Effective Conflict Resolution

1. Listen Actively: Approach conflicts with a willingness to listen and understand. Give your partner the space to express their thoughts and feelings without interruption.

2. Express Feelings Calmly: Communicate your own feelings and perspective calmly and respectfully. Avoid using accusatory language and focus on using "I" statements to convey your emotions.

3. Seek Understanding: Strive to understand your partner's point of view before seeking to be understood. Empathize with their feelings and

acknowledge their perspective.

4. Focus on Solutions: Approach conflicts as problems to be solved rather than assigning blame. Collaborate with your partner to brainstorm solutions that address both parties' needs.

5. Take Breaks if Needed: If conflicts become heated, consider taking a break to cool down before continuing the conversation. This prevents escalating emotions and allows for a more productive discussion later.

Fostering Unity Through Communication

In conclusion, this chapter emphasizes the instrumental role of friendship in nurturing effective communication and conflict resolution within romantic relationships. By fostering open conversations, active listening, and a friend's perspective in addressing conflicts, partners create an environment of empathy and understanding. The friendship-based foundation paves the way for collaboration, mutual respect, and unity, allowing partners to communicate openly and navigate conflicts with compassion, reinforcing the very essence of enduring companionship and love.

12

Embracing the Friendship-Romance Connection

A Tapestry Woven with Friendship and Love: Reflecting on the Journey

As we conclude our exploration of friendship-based romantic relationships, it's an opportune time to reflect on the remarkable journey of discovering the profound interplay between friendship and love. This chapter encapsulates the essence of this connection, summarizing the key takeaways and offering guidance on how to nurture and sustain the friendship within romantic partnerships.

The Journey of Discovery

The journey through these chapters has unveiled the multifaceted nature of friendship-based romantic relationships. We've explored how friendship underpins the emotional foundation of these partnerships, enriching connections, and fostering unity. We've delved into the ways in which shared interests, open communication, empathy, and a sense of adventure contribute to a bond that deepens with time. We've celebrated the art of balancing togetherness and independence, navigating challenges, and embracing personal growth.

This journey of discovery has illuminated the integral role that friendship plays in shaping the love that thrives within these relationships. It has underscored the importance of viewing each other as companions, confidants, and allies on a shared journey of growth and evolution.

Key Takeaways

1. Friendship as a Foundation: Friendship provides a steady foundation upon which romantic love can flourish. By cultivating trust, emotional intimacy, and a sense of companionship, partners create a bond that is resilient and enduring.

2. Effective Communication: Open and honest communication is a hallmark of both friendships and romantic relationships. Sharing thoughts, feelings, and concerns openly creates an atmosphere of understanding and empathy.

3. Empathy and Emotional Support: Partners who offer emotional support and empathy create a safe space for vulnerability and growth. This fosters a connection that is rooted in mutual understanding and unity.

4. Shared Experiences and Adventure: Engaging in shared interests and embarking on new experiences infuses relationships with excitement and joy. These shared memories become touchstones that enrich the bond.

5. Balancing Togetherness and Independence: Striking a balance between spending time together and nurturing individual interests promotes a dynamic, harmonious relationship that respects both partners' autonomy.

Guidance for Nurturing Friendship in Relationships

1. Prioritize Quality Time: Spend meaningful time together, engaging in shared activities that nurture emotional connection and communication.

2. Stay Playful: Infuse playfulness and humor into your interactions to keep the relationship lighthearted and vibrant.

3. Communicate Openly: Embrace open communication to foster transparency, understanding, and mutual support.

4. Support Individual Growth: Encourage and celebrate each other's personal growth and aspirations, creating a partnership that thrives on shared evolution.

5. Navigate Challenges Together: Approach challenges with a united front, drawing from the support and empathy characteristic of friendships.

6. Cultivate a Sense of Adventure: Continuously seek out new experiences and share adventures to keep the relationship dynamic and exciting.

7. Celebrate Milestones: Acknowledge and celebrate the milestones in your relationship, reinforcing the journey you've taken together.

A Continual Journey

As we conclude this journey through the connection between friendship and romance, remember that the essence of friendship in relationships is an ongoing endeavor. It requires dedication, patience, and a commitment to nurturing the emotional connection that underpins lasting love. By embracing the lessons learned and continuing to prioritize the friendship within your romantic partnership, you embark on a journey of companionship, growth, and enduring unity—a journey enriched by the threads of friendship and love woven into the very fabric of your relationship.

Conclusion: The Friendship That Anchors Love

In the intricate dance of romantic relationships, one thread shines with particular brilliance—the thread of friendship. Through the journey we've embarked upon, we've explored the profound impact of friendship on love, uncovering the ways in which it strengthens the very foundation of our partnerships. As we conclude this exploration, let us reinforce the notion that friendship is the cornerstone upon which enduring and vibrant romantic connections are built.

The Unbreakable Bond of Friendship

Friendship is more than a label; it is a dynamic force that breathes life into relationships. It's the camaraderie that blossoms when partners view each other as confidants, allies, and kindred spirits. It's the safety net of trust and open communication that catches us when we stumble, guiding us through the challenges that life presents. It's the shared laughter, the empathy, and the unspoken understanding that deepens our connection.

Our journey has shown us that the bond of friendship enriches every facet of a romantic relationship. From shared interests and adventures that infuse joy into our lives, to the empathy and emotional support that sustain us during tough times, friendship's fingerprints are found on every moment, every memory, and every triumph we experience together.

Prioritizing and Celebrating Friendship

As we reflect on the chapters that have unfolded, let us remember that the friendship-based aspect of our relationships is not just a passive presence—it's an active force that deserves our attention and nurturing. The lessons we've learned guide us toward fostering unity through autonomy, embracing vulnerability, and navigating challenges with unity and understanding.

Let us encourage each other to embrace the lessons we've uncovered and to prioritize the friendship within our romantic partnerships. Just as we celebrate milestones of love, let us also take time to celebrate the milestones of friendship—those moments of shared joy, the triumphs over adversity, and the growth we've experienced side by side.

A Continuous Journey

Our exploration may be concluding, but our journey continues. The friendship that strengthens our romantic relationships is not a static concept; it's a living, breathing connection that requires our attention, dedication, and care. Let's continue to cultivate an environment where trust, communication, empathy, and shared growth flourish.

As we move forward, let's remember that the friendship aspect of our relationships isn't just a stepping stone—it's the very essence that anchors our love. Let's honor it, cherish it, and let it guide us as we navigate the paths of life together, celebrating not only the love we share but also the friendship that makes it enduring, enriching, and eternally vibrant.

www.ingramcontent.com/pod-product-compliance
Lightning Source LLC
LaVergne TN
LVHW020738090526
838202LV00057BA/5986